25¢

"Rock of Ages" Sermon Outlines

"Rock of Ages" Sermon Outlines

Russell E. Spray

PULPIT LIBRARY

BAKER BOOK HOUSE Grand Rapids, Michigan 49506

Copyright 1983 by
Baker Book House Company
ISBN: 0-8010-8235-8

Printed in the United States of America

Table of Contents

Foreword 5
1. "Rock of Ages" .... I. COR. 10:4 6
2. The Works of the D-E-V-I-L .. I JOHN. 3:8 8
3. Categorizing Christians .... II. PET. ER. 2:11 10
4. Discipline Your Life ...... I COR: 9:27 12
5. Feeding the Multitude .... MARK. 6:42 14
6. When Patience Is Needed .... LUKE 21:19 16
7. How Christians Should T-A-L-K .. JAMES 3:13 18
8. You Can Preach the Gospel .... MARK. 16:15 20
9. How to Conquer Inferiority Feelings .. PHIL. 4:13 ... 22
10. How to Cope with Trials ... I. PETER 1:7 24
11. How to Live Victoriously ... I. COR. 15:57 26
12. L-I-F-T Up Your Eyes ...... JOHN. 4:35 28
13. Overcoming Your F-E-A-R-S .... PS. 27:1 30
14. Secret Prayer ...... MATT. 6:6 32
15. Spiritual Millionaires .... ROM. 11:33 34
16. Tests to Determine God's Will . EPH. 5:17 36
17. How to Win Over S-E-L-F ... MATT. 16:24 38
18. The Face of Jesus .... MATT. 17:4 40
19. The Love of Money .... I. TIM. 6:10 42
20. How to L-E-A-N on Jesus .. I. PETER 5:7 44
21. The Prodigal Son .... LUKE 15:24 46
22. The Road to Spiritual Success .. JOSH. 1:8 48
23. Your Life Is a Voyage .... PS. 107:30 50
24. M-O-S-E-S .... EXOD: 4:12 52
25. Stop Fretting .... PS. 37:1 54
26. The Bible Speaks .... PS. 119:133 56
27. This Is the Year (New Year's) .. LUKE 4:18-19 58

Foreword

"They drank of that spiritual Rock that followed them: and that Rock was Christ." (I Cor. 10:4)

These sermon outlines are intended to point the lost to Christ and to encourage Christians. I pray that all who use and hear them will be especially blessed by Christ, the "Rock of Ages."

Russell E. Spray

1

"Rock of Ages"

"They drank of that spiritual Rock that followed them: and that Rock was Christ" (I Cor. 10:4).

Christ, the "Rock of Ages," is "the same yesterday, and to day, and for ever" (Heb. 13:8).

I. Rock of Redemption

"Thou art . . . the rock of my salvation" (Ps. 89:26).

  A. Verse 1 of the hymn, "Rock of Ages": "Rock of Ages! cleft for me,/ Let me hide myself in Thee./ Let the water and the blood/ From Thy wounded side which flowed,/ Be of sin the double cure,/ Save from wrath and make me pure."
  B. Many search for peace of mind through medicine, science, drugs, drink, possessions, and pleasures, but fail to find peace in any of these.
  C. Christ is the Rock of Redemption. He lifts up the penitent soul and frees him from guilt and the bondage of sin.
  D. Christians who totally commit their life to Christ are cleansed and made spiritually whole, empowered for service, and enabled to meet life's challenges (Ps. 62:6-7).

II. Rock of Restoration

"He brought me up also out of an horrible pit . . . and set my feet upon a rock . . . " (Ps. 40:2).

  A. Verse 2 of the hymn, "Rock of Ages": "Could my tears forever flow,/ Could my zeal no languor know,/ These for sin could not atone:/ Thou must save, and Thou alone;/ In my hand no price I bring,/ Simply to Thy cross I cling."
  B. Silver and gold cannot buy forgiveness; kings and presidents cannot atone for sins. Christ's death on the cross

paid the penalty for sin and restored man's fellowship with God.

C. Christ is the Rock of Restoration for the burdened, troubled, and lonely. When worries and troubles abound, He is our shelter and hiding place.

D. When we become exhausted by frenzied activity, Christ is "as the shadow of a great rock in a weary land" (Isa. 32:2). He restores those who trust Him.

III. Rock of Revelation

"Lead me to the rock that is higher than I" (Ps. 61:2).

A. Verse 3 of the hymn, "Rock of Ages": "While I draw this fleeting breath,/ When my eyes shall close in death,/ When I rise to worlds unknown,/ And behold Thee on Thy throne,/ Rock of Ages! cleft for me!/ Let me hide myself in Thee."

B. Christ is with Christians at home, at work, and at play. Christians need not fear death, for He has promised never to leave nor forsake His own (Heb. 13:5).

C. There are many things in this life that we do not understand. We often ask "Why?" Christ is the Rock of Revelation. He will enlighten us in our life to come.

D. Salvation provides the means for us to live a fulfilled and purposeful life here on earth, and assures us of a far greater (and everlasting) life after death. Christ is our Rock of Redemption and Restoration in this life and the Rock of Revelation in the life to come. He is the "Rock of Ages" (I Cor. 2:9).

2

The Works of the D-E-V-I-L

"For this purpose the Son of God was manifested, that he might destroy the works of the devil" (I John 3:8).

By becoming aware and knowledgeable concerning the works of the D-E-V-I-L, we will increase our faith, assuring victory.

I. D-eceitfulness
"Satan . . . shall go out to deceive the nations" (Rev. 20:7-8).
- A. The devil constantly tries to deceive God's people. He attempts to make wrong appear right and right appear wrong.
- B. In our quest for victory we must test our activities by the Word of God. We must also pray and depend on the Holy Spirit for direction (Matt. 24:24). He never fails.

II. E-nviousness
"Let us not be desirous of vain glory . . . envying one another" (Gal. 5:26).
- A. Satan tempts Christians to envy others. Envy engenders strife, jealousy, division, and resentment, causing trouble in the home, church, and world.
- B. We must seek God's approval for our lives. We win over envy by exercising love and compassion for others (James 3:14-17).

III. V-iciousness
"The devil, as a roaring lion, walketh about, seeking whom he may devour" (I Peter 5:8).

A. Satan is malicious and violent. Riots, robberies, rapes, and murders are common in our society (Gal. 5:20-21).
B. The devil uses drastic ways to try to defeat God's people. Yet God is more than a match for Satan. We are conquerors through God (Rom. 8:37).

IV. I-dolatry

". . . *my dearly beloved, flee from idolatry" (I Cor. 10:14).*

A. In our modern affluent society millions place their love in money, real estate, and investments. Their time, talents, and finances are centered on temporal gain.
B. Our activities and affections must be centered on God. He knows our needs and has promised to supply them (Matt. 6:33).

V. L-ewdness

"The works of the flesh are . . . Adultery, fornication, uncleanness, lasciviousness" (Gal. 5:19).

A. The devil often uses sexual desire to capture unsuspecting souls. He employs illicit sex—adultery, fornication, homosexuality—in his pursuits.
B. Be on guard against the lusts of the flesh. Focus on the fruit of the Spirit and in exercising these in doing God's work. God's work always brings victory over the works of the devil (Gal. 5:22-24).

3

Categorizing Christians

"Seeing then that all these things shall be dissolved, what manner of persons ought ye to be in all holy conversation and godliness" (II Peter 3:11).

Christians fall into different categories. Where do you fit in?

I. Sleeping Christians
"Awake thou that sleepest, and arise from the dead, and Christ shall give thee light" (Eph. 5:14).
   A. Sleeping Christians seem unaware of the spiritual needs of others and thus say or do nothing that might promote God's kingdom. These Christians are not growing spiritually.
   B Many Christians are alert when it comes to personal interests, possessions, and pleasure but are lethargic about working for God.
   C. Christ warned Christians to awaken from their spiritual sleep and become alive to the things of the Spirit (Eph. 5:14-19).

II. Sulking Christians
"Be no more children . . . but speaking the truth in love, . . . grow up into him in all things . . . " (Eph. 4:14-15).
   A. Sulkiness is "showing resentment and ill-humor by sullen, withdrawn behavior . . . gloomy, dismal, sullen"—Webster.
   B. Some Christians are overly sensitive, easily hurt, sulky. They hold resentments and require constant attention. They fail to put away childish things (I Cor. 13:11).
   C. We must care about others' rights, feelings, and needs. We

need to "grow in grace, and in the knowledge of our Lord and Saviour Jesus Christ" (II Peter 3:18).

III. Slamming Christians

"Study to be quiet, and to do your own business . . ."
(I Thess. 4:11).

- A. Some Christians stir up trouble because they are inwardly ill at ease. They are often loud, abusive, and insensitive to the rights and feelings of others.
- B. Slamming Christians criticize and find fault easily. They are seldom content with what others do.
- C. We must do unto others as we would have others to do unto us (Matt. 7:12). Loving God and giving Him first place will enable us to love others with regard and respect.

IV. Serving Christians

"Labour not for the meat which perisheth, but for that meat which endureth unto everlasting life . . ." (John 6:27).

- A. Serving Christians do not seek the honor of man but strive to glorify God and be a blessing to others.
- B. Serving Christians are happy Christians. They are too big-hearted to be little, too broad-minded to be narrow. They build God's kingdom here on earth.
- C. Am I sleeping, sulking, slamming, or serving? "I must work the works of him that sent me, while it is day: the night cometh, when no man can work" (John 9:4).

4

Discipline Your Life

"But I keep under my body, and bring it into subjection: lest that by any means, when I have preached to others, I myself should be a castaway" (I Cor. 9:27)

Discipline is necessary for success in any endeavor. It is needed most, however, for success in our daily living.

I. Discipline Your Thinking
"Bring into captivity every thought to the obedience of Christ" (II Cor. 10:5).
- A. Many Christians are in bondage to evil and negative thoughts. Struggling to be free of these undesirable thoughts only causes them to linger.
- B. Evil and negative thoughts must be replaced with good and positive ones. Keeping one's mind filled with good crowds out the bad. "Think on these things" (Phil. 4:8).

II. Discipline Your Hearing
"Incline your ear . . . hear, and your soul shall live" (Isa. 55:3).
- A. The media today are flooded with foul language, suggestiveness, slander, and smut.
- B. Christians should discipline their hearing by listening to what the Lord says through His Word. They need also to lend a listening ear to the cries of the lonely, discouraged, depressed, and the lost (Rom. 10:17).

III. Discipline Your Seeing
"Looking unto Jesus the author and finisher of our faith" (Heb. 12:2).
- A. Christians should strive to see the good, not the faults and failures in others. Christians should limit their exposure to the lust and violence that television and the movies present.

B. We must keep our eyes on Jesus (Isa. 40:26). What would He have us view?

IV. Discipline Your Talking
"For by thy words thou shalt be justified, and by thy words thou shalt be condemned" (Matt. 12:37).
- A. Harsh and critical words are destructive. Kind and understanding words bring healing. "A soft answer turneth away wrath: but grievous words stir up anger" (Prov. 15:1).
- B. Disciplined words produce blessings and give witness to Christ (Prov. 15:23).

V. Discipline Your Doing
"In every good work to do his will . . ." (Heb. 13:21).
- A. Failure to do God's work often results from too much busyness, lack of concern, or inferiority feelings.
- B. We must make and take time for God. Prayer, Bible study, and doing good works not only encourage us but they bless others and bring glory to God (I Tim. 6:18-19).

VI. Discipline Your Going
"As ye have therefore received Christ Jesus the Lord, so walk ye in him" (Col. 2:6).
- A. People today are constantly on the go, trying to satisfy their inner longings and discontent by keeping busy.
- B. Real joy and contentment are found only in Jesus Christ. We must be faithful in church attendance and witnessing. If we go for God, He will go with us (Josh. 1:9).

5

Feeding the Multitude

"And they did all eat, and were filled" (Mark 6:42).

Jesus Christ is the same today as He was in times past. He still works miracles for those who trust and obey.

I. The Compassion (Mark 6:30-34)
"And Jesus . . . was moved with compassion toward them, because they were as sheep not having a shepherd" (Mark 6:34).
- A. Millions today are "as sheep not having a shepherd." They are seeking something to satisfy the hunger and longing of their souls.
- B. Jesus is the same today. He is still "moved with compassion" for the multitudes who are lost and scattered.
- C. Christ's power is the same, but He chooses to work through us. Why are today's multitudes not fed? Have we failed? Has the church failed?

II. The Complaints (Mark 6:35-37)
"This is a desert place . . . Send them away . . . for they have nothing to eat" (Mark 6:35-36).
- A. The complaints came from the disciples, but Jesus, disregarding their murmurings, performed a miracle.
- B. There are many complainers in the churches. They find fault with the way things are done and the way things are not done.
- C. We must disregard the complaints as Jesus did. If we keep on praying, believing, and working, miracles will happen.

III. The Command (Mark 6:38-40)

"And he commanded them to make all sit down by companies upon the grass" (Mark 6:39).

- A. When the complainers obeyed the Master's command, good things began to happen.
- B. When we rid ourselves of selfish motives, envy, strife, and resentment, we can be part of the solution, not the problem.
- C. Faultfinders can help bring miracles to pass just like the disciples did—if they obey the Lord's command.

IV. The Conquest (Mark 6:41-44)

"He looked up to heaven, and blessed, and brake the loaves . . . and the two fishes. . . . And they did all eat, and were filled" (Mark 6:41-42).

- A. Everyone worked together in harmony with the Master and the miracle happened. "They did all eat, and were filled."
- B. We must forgive ourselves and others, forget the past, and totally commit our lives to God, then love and work together in unity.
- C. Churches and individuals who are obedient and exercise faith can be victorious in Jesus Christ today. He still feeds the multitudes.

6

When Patience Is Needed

"In your patience possess ye your souls" (Luke 21:19).

Patience is needed in all of life. We learn patience through practice, perseverance, and God's help. The following should help us gain in patience.

I. Waiting Requires Patience
"Rest in the LORD, and wait patiently for him . . ."
(Ps. 37:7).
- A. Waiting can be most difficult. We want to see results immediately, but we must learn to wait for God's time.
- B. God's timing is never premature and never too late. It takes time for God to grow an oak tree or a rose.
- C. It also takes time for God to answer certain of our prayers. We must wait patiently, with faith, knowing His plan and purpose are best (Ps. 40:1).

II. Working Requires Patience
"Knowing this, that the trying of your faith worketh patience"
(James 1:3).
- A. Patience is needed when working with others. We must be considerate of their rights and differences of opinion.
- B. We must surrender to God's will. His way is superior to our own.
- C. God's work bears fruit in His time. When results are slow in coming, we must patiently continue to work (Col. 3:23-24).

III. Winning Requires Patience

". . . let us run with patience the race that is set before us" (Heb. 12:1).

   A. Winning the Christian race is vitally important. Winning doesn't come by luck or chance but by practice and endurance.
   B. Patience and perseverance are necessities. Winning Christians must keep on believing, praying, and working.
   C. Patience is needed when others misjudge our motives. Man looks on the outward appearance but God on the heart (I Sam. 16:7).

IV. Waning Requires Patience

"For ye have need of patience, that, after ye have done the will of God, ye might receive the promise" (Heb. 10:36).

   A. Misfortune, sickness, and aging often bring a decline in power and prosperity. They may also tempt us to discouragement and defeat.
   B. The best is yet to come for those who keep on praying, trusting, and obeying. God has a purpose in what He allows.
   C. We must wait patiently, assured that everything will work together for our good and God's glory (Rom. 8:28).

7

How Christians Should T-A-L-K

"Who is a wise man and endued with knowledge among you? Let him shew out of a good conversation his works with meekness of wisdom" (James 3:13).

How Christians T-A-L-K is very important. Their words can help or hurt their influence. They should speak:

I. T-ruthfully

"*But speaking the truth in love . . ." (Eph. 4:15).*

- A. Dishonesty is so prevalent today that is is often difficult to distinguish between truth and untruth.
- B. To speak the truth doesn't mean we must tell everything we know about people or situations. It simply means that what we do say should be reliable and accurate.
- C. Christians should avoid criticizing and faultfinding. They should look for the good, not the bad, and speak "the truth in love" (Eph. 4:15).

II. A-greeably

"Can two walk together, except they be agreed?" (Amos 3:3).

- A. Some people are defiant, invariably taking the opposite point of view. They should realize that one can disagree in an agreeable way.
- B. Christians should be as agreeable as possible, so long as an issue doesn't violate their convictions.
- C. If we are to be a blessing and win others to Christ, we must heed Paul's admonition: "As much as lieth in you, live peaceably with all men" (Rom. 12:18).

III. L-ovingly

"Speak not evil one of another . . ." (James 4:11).

A. Some people have difficulty giving others compliments and encouragement. Their lack of expression may be based on a low self-image.
B. When we give words of love and appreciation to others, we often find our own sagging ego is lifted.
C. Christians must put into the practice the adage: "If you can't say something good about another, don't say anything at all" (See I Peter 3:8-10).

IV. K-indly

"And be ye kind one to another, tenderhearted, forgiving one another . . ." (Eph. 4:32).

A. All people, however sophisticated or crude, educated or uneducated, young or old, rich or poor, need love, kindness, and understanding.
B. Love, kindness, and understanding should govern our talk. Unkind words that take no thought for a person's feelings should not be spoken.
C. "Be kindly affectioned one to another with brotherly love; in honour preferring one another" (Rom. 12:10). Kind words reap weighty dividends.

8

You Can Preach the Gospel

"And he said unto them, Go ye into all the world, and preach the gospel to every creature" (Mark 16:15).

Preaching the gospel is not reserved for the called-of-God ministers only. Each Chrisitan can preach the gospel in God's chosen way for him.

I. Speak It

"For it is not ye that speak, but the Spirit of your Father which speaketh in you" (Matt. 10:20).

A. You may not be a great orator or speak eloquently, but you can still preach the gospel in God's chosen way for you.

B. People are full of idle talk. Christians ought all to abound in talk about the things of the Lord.

C. We should believe that God is speaking through us in whatever we say, wherever we may be (Ps. 26:7).

II. Sing It

"Serve the Lord with gladness: come before his presence with singing" (Ps. 100:2).

A. Every good song has a message. Those who spread the gospel in song are not only blessed but are a blessing as well.

B. Everyone can make a joyful noise unto the Lord. Joy is attractive and people go where they can find it.

C. Christians should always have a song in their heart and give expression to it. Others will want the joy of the Lord that Christians exude (Ps. 104:33).

III. Send It

"He sendeth forth his commandment upon earth: his word runneth very swiftly" (Ps. 147:15).

A. The gospel reaches many through Christian writers.
B. Those who cannot write for publication can send the gospel message via their financial support.
C. All Christians can send up prayers to God who loves to receive and answer our prayers. He sends supplies, support, and salvation in response (Isa. 55:1).

IV. Share It

"As every man hath received the gift, even so minister the same one to another" (I Peter 4:10).

A. Sharing is one of the first lessons children should be taught. Sharing helps them grow up to be unselfish.
B. Christians must share Christ with others. We cannot keep Him to ourselves. The gospel is "to every creature."
C. We preach to the poor and needy when we feed and clothe them. We preach to the bereaved and lonely when we comfort them. We preach to the unsaved when we share Christ's forgiveness and cleansing (Mark 16:15).

9

How to Conquer Inferiority Feelings

"I can do all things through Christ which strengtheneth me" (Phil. 4:13).

Many Christians suffer frustration because of inferiority feelings. They fail to glorify God as they should and be the blessing they could be. To overcome inferiority feelings:

I. Be Conscious of God

"The Spirit . . . beareth witness with our spirit, that we are the children of God" (Rom. 8:16).

A. Far too many Christians are self-conscious rather than God-conscious. They betray themselves with their "me first, me second, and me last" attitude.

B. We must get self off the throne and give God first place. We must practice the presence of God by fellowshiping with Him at all times.

C. Deliberate action is needed. We conquer by becoming involved in the burdens, needs, cares, suffering, and concerns of others, doing all to the glory of God (Rom. 14:8).

II. Be Committed to God

"He is able to keep that which I have committed unto him against that day" (II Tim. 1:12).

A. When it comes to total commitment, many Christians resist. They reserve a portion of their life for selfish purposes.

B. The lack of total commitment brings doubt, fear, insecurity. God is able to keep only "that which I have committed unto him."

C. When we completely surrender our will to God, we are set free of self. He bears the responsibility for our life.

III. Be Confident in God

"And the effect of righteousness shall be quietness and assurance for ever" (Isa. 32:17).

A. Too many Christians are searching for self-confidence rather than God-confidence. They lack the inner strength to cope.
B. Finite power falters but God's infinite power never fails. Inferiority feelings lose their grip as Christians gain confidence in God.
C. God's promises delivered Jeremiah. "Be not afraid of their faces: for I am with thee to deliver thee, saith the LORD" (Jer. 1:18). He is with us today.

IV. Be Controlled by God

"And we know that in all things God works for the good of those who love him" (Rom. 8:28, NIV).

A. Some Christians try to lift their sagging ego by usurping authority over others.
B. When God is in complete control, we need not be plagued with low self-esteem and inferiority feelings.
C. The God-controlled Christian hails Him as King of Kings and Lord of Lords. He is our heavenly Father and we are His children, "heirs of God, and joint-heirs with Christ" (Rom. 8:17).

10

How to Cope with Trials

"That the trial of your faith . . . though it be tried with fire, might be found unto praise and honour and glory at the appearing of Jesus Christ" (I Peter 1:7).

Trials come to everyone. We can better cope with them if we do the following.

I. Radiate God's Presence

"For he hath said, I will never leave thee, nor forsake thee" (Heb. 13:5).

A. When trials strike, some Christians look and act like they have lost their last friend because they fail to fellowship with God as they should.

B. Negative attitudes depress oneself, discourage others, and displease God. During trials, we must exercise positive attitudes and live by faith.

C. Radiating God's presence, we testify to others of God's grace. When we draw near to God, He is present to help us cope with trials (James 4:8).

II. Remember God's Promises

"When thou passest through the waters . . . they shall not overflow thee" (Isa. 43:2).

A. Jesus used the Word of God to combat temptation: "It is written." When we are faced with testings and trials, we must follow His example.

B. God's promises extend to all our human needs. We have only to find the promise that fits our area of concern and claim it as our own.

C. Reading God's promises is not enough, we must accept and keep them in mind. They will help us cope in times of trial (II Peter 1:4).

III. Recognize God's Purpose

"All things work together for good to them that love God" (Rom. 8:28).

A. God has a purpose in all He allows to come to His children. Don't become so upset over a trial that you overlook God's purpose.
B. Christians often complain bitterly under testing. "How can this possibly be for my good?" They need to surrender to God's will.
C. God's will is best. He knows that what, when, where, why, and how to "make you perfect, stablish, strengthen, settle you" (I Peter 5:10).

IV. Rely on God's Power

"He giveth power to the faint; and to them that have no might he increaseth strength" (Isa. 40:29).

A. When trials assail, too many Christians rely on their own strength. They flounder and fail.
B. Man's finite power cannot cope with today's problems, but God's infinite power is sufficient for our needs.
C. We must trust, lean, and depend on God's omnipotent power. His promise is: "I will strengthen . . . I will help . . . I will uphold thee with the right hand of my righteousness" (Isa. 41:10).

11

How to Live Victoriously

"But thanks be to God, which giveth us the victory through our Lord Jesus Christ" (I Cor. 15:57).

Many Christians fail to live victoriously. They struggle through life, often plagued by discouragement and defeat. To live victoriously we must:

I. Learn from God's Scripture

"Written for our learning, that we through . . . the scriptures might have hope" (Rom. 15:4).

- A. Christians who fail to read God's Word are seldom victorious. They are easy prey to depression.
- B. The Scriptures teach us to "hope thou in God." They show us the way from sin to salvation, from stress to serenity, from remorse to rejoicing.
- C. We must be diligent to learn God's Word. Victory is assured those who memorize the promises, believe them, and claim them for their own (II Cor. 1:20).

II. Lean on God's Strength

"He giveth power to the faint; and to them that hath no might he increaseth strength" (Isa. 40:29).

- A. Many Christians act as if they are carrying the burdens of the world on their shoulders.
- B. Finite strength is insufficient. Those who depend on it falter and fall under the loads they carry.
- C. God's infinite power always prevails. He is able to lift any load, carry any burden, and set captives free. Live victoriously—lean on God's strength (Isa. 41:10).

III. Labor in God's Service

"Labour . . . for that meat which endureth unto everlasting life . . ." (John 6:27).

  A. Christians often suffer defeat because they do not become involved in God's service as they should.
  B. They spend their time, effort, and resources in selfish pursuits and personal gain. They have their reward. We are to lay up treasures in heaven, not here on earth (Matt. 6:19-21).
  C. Involvement in church activities, assisting the less fortunate, lifting the downhearted, and sharing Christ brings victory now and eternal rewards in the future.

IV. Love Through God's Spirit

"Obeying the truth through the Spirit unto unfeigned love of the brethren . . ." (I Peter 1:22).

  A. Millions sustain loss because God's love is lacking in individuals, homes, churches, and the world at large.
  B. Love is a built-in psychological and spiritual need. Our greatest need is not for more power or possessions, but for more love. It brings satisfaction and fulfillment.
  C. We must ask God to fill us with His love. The more love we have, the less fear, resentment, and strife we possess (I John 4:18).

12

L-I-F-T Up Your Eyes

"Lift up your eyes, and look on the fields; for they are white already to harvest" (John 4:35).

Christians should not become complacent about God's work. Laborers are needed. The fields are "white unto harvest." L-I-F-T up your eyes and . . .

I. L-ook

"Look on the fields; for they are white already to harvest" (John 4:35).

   A. Ours is a pleasure-mad world. Many live to have a good time, trying to fill the emptiness in their lives with varied entertainments.
   B. We must look to Jesus. He alone can satisfy the longing of the soul (Heb. 12:2).
   C. Christians must look with compassion on the lost, being faithful to witness to them of the saving and cleansing power of Jesus Christ.

II. I-nvest

"Lay up for yourselves treasures in heaven . . ." (Matt. 6:20).

   A. Many people invest in houses and land, cars and boats, gadgets galore. Temporal things do not last.
   B. To those who give God first place in their life, He has promised that "all these things shall be added unto" them (Matt. 6:33).
   C. We must invest in spiritual treasures by faithful attendance to worship, financially supporting the church, and diligently sharing Christ with the unsaved. These are of eternal value.

III. F-orbear

"Forbearing one another in love" (Eph. 4:2).

A. To forbear one another in love means there is no holding of resentments, that there is a readiness to forgive, "for [love] shall cover the multitude of sins" (I Peter 4:8).

B. Those who forbear one another in love are ready to visit the sick and lonely, comfort the discouraged and troubled, and extend a helping hand to the needy, sharing Christ with all.

IV. T-riumph

"He that goeth forth and weepeth, bearing precious seed, shall doubtless come again with rejoicing, bringing his sheaves with him" (Ps. 126:6).

A. Reaching out to others may be difficult at times. It may bring refusals, rejections, and rebuffs, but we must not "be weary in well doing" (Gal. 6:9a).

B. We must continue praying, trusting, and working when the odds are against us, "for in due season we shall reap, if we faint not" (Gal. 6:9b).

C. If we look with compassion, invest in eternal values, and forbear one another in love, we shall triumph in both this life and the life to come.

13

Overcoming Your F-E-A-R-S

"The LORD is my light and my salvation; whom shall I fear? the LORD is the strength of my life; of whom shall I be afraid? (Ps. 27:1).

Satan uses fear to stifle and defeat God's people. Christians can overcome their F-E-A-R-S through:

I. F-aith

"Be not afraid, only believe" (Mark 5:36).

A. Faith is the antidote for fear. To overcome we must replace our fears with confidence in God.
B. When the disciples were driven by the storm and feared for their lives, Jesus "rebuked the wind . . . and there was a great calm" (Mark 4:39). He still asks today, "Why are ye so fearful? how is it that ye have no faith?" (Mark 4:40).

II. E-ndurance

"Though an host . . . encamp against me, my heart shall not fear" (Ps. 27:3).

A. The psalmist was often terrorized by wicked and sinful men, but he endured and overcame through faith, trust, and dependence on the Lord.
B. Our world today is also a world of violence, demanding perseverance and endurance (II Tim. 2:3). By putting our complete trust in God, as the psalmist did, we too can overcome our fears.

III. A-ffection

"Perfect love casteth out fear" (I John 4:18).

A. Resentment causes Christians to be fearful. More love is needed (II Tim. 1:7).

B. Love is increased by praying for others, performing good deeds, and showing kindness. God is love. The more of Him we have, the less fear we possess. "There is no fear in love" (I John 4:18).

IV. R-eliance

"What time I am afraid, I will trust in thee" (Ps. 56:3).

A. Some Christians rely on self-effort. Others rely on doctors, lawyers, friends, and modern-day science. But finite strength is insufficient for our needs.

B. We must depend upon God's infinite power. He never fails. When we trust Him implicitly, we can say with the psalmist, "The LORD is the strength of my life; of whom shall I be afraid?" (Ps. 27:1).

V. S-ervice

"The Lord is my helper, and I will not fear what man shall do unto me" (Heb. 13:6).

A. We overcome the fear of failure through activity. Working for God brings satisfaction and a sense of accomplishment.

B. We need not tackle God's work alone. He is our helper. "We [are] workers together with him . . ." (II Cor. 6:1).

C. Service for God brings a reward now and in the life to come. We overcome our earthly fears and we lay up treasures in heaven, where all fear has vanished away (Rev. 21:7).

14

Secret Prayer

"But thou, when thou prayest, enter into thy closet, and when thou hast shut thy door, pray to thy Father which is in secret; and thy Father . . . shall reward thee openly" (Matt. 6:6).

Prayer is the privilege of all Christians. To come to a better understanding about secret prayer, let us consider the following.

I. The Period of Secret Prayer
   "But thou, when thou prayest . . ." (Matt. 6:6).
   A. Most people make time for the things they truly want to do. They spare little expense and sacrifice to accomplish these activities.
   B. Christians should be diligent about fellowshipping with God. They should set aside a time for prayer daily.
   C. We must give God first place in our lives. When we do, we can claim the promise: "All these things shall be added unto you" (Matt. 6:33).

II. The Place of Secret Prayer
   "Enter into thy closet, and when thou hast shut thy door . . ." (Matt. 6:6).
   A. A place of solitude is desirable for prayer. This, however, is not always possible in our busy society.
   B. Christians must learn to pray everywhere—on the way to work, during working hours, and even in the midst of traffic (I Thess. 5:17).
   C. With practice Christians can "shut the door" to worry and strife and be uplifted and calmed as they fellowship with God (Luke 18:1).

III. The Person of Secret Prayer

"Pray to thy Father which is in secret" (Matt. 6:6).

A. Many erroneously believe that it doesn't matter to whom they pray as long as they are sincere. There is but one true God to whom we must pray in Jesus' name.

B. Our prayers should not be vague and indefinite. We must be specific, bringing our petitions to God by name and in faith.

C. We must praise our heavenly Father for answered prayer. Praise Him for what He has done, what He is doing, and what He is going to do (Eph. 5:20).

IV. The Prize of Secret Prayer

"Thy Father which seeth in secret shall reward thee openly" (Matt. 6:6).

A. Praying Christians are rewarded in this life. They possess a joy and purpose for living that others do not.

B. The confidence and assurance manifested by praying Christians will cause others to want to become Christians also.

C. The prize is not limited to this life alone but extends into the next. The best is yet to come for praying Christians who shall "ever be with the Lord" (I Thess. 4:17).

15

Spiritual Millionaires

"O the depth of the riches both of the wisdom and knowledge of God! how unsearchable are his judgments, and his ways past finding out" (Rom. 11:33).

Most people desire riches, but some things are more valuable than money. Christians can be "spiritual millionaires."

I. Rich in Faith

"Hath not God chosen the poor of this world rich in faith . . ." (James 2:5).

- A. The value of faith is incalculable. We are saved by faith, sanctified by faith, and sustained by faith (Rom. 8:17).
- B. Many Christians face spiritual bankruptcy because they lack faith. Haunted by doubts and fears, they live beneath their privilege as servants of Christ Jesus (Mark 4:40).
- C. God wants His children to be rich in faith (Mark 11:24). We gain faith by praying as the apostles did—"Lord, increase our faith" (Luke 17:5).
- D. We also gain faith by using the faith we have. The more we work our faith, the more our faith works for us (James 2:14-26).

II. Rich in Hope

"Being justified by his grace, we should be made heirs according to the hope of eternal life" (Titus 3:7).

- A. Hope is necessary to life. It brings physical healing. It lifts the mind out of discouragement, despondency, and depression (Ps. 42:5, 11).

B. Hope brings spiritual healing to all sinners.
C. Hope is gained by replacing negative thinking with positive thoughts, fearful thoughts with faithful thoughts. We must look for the good, not the bad.
D. Hope is also gained by action. We must not only think good thoughts but we must do good deeds, thus bringing help to others, honor to God, and "hope of eternal life" to us (Titus 1:2).

III. Rich in Love

"God, who is rich in mercy, for his great love wherewith he loved us" (Eph. 2:4).

A. Faith and hope are necessary to salvation, serenity, and sustenance. We cannot live without them.
B. Love is also a psychological and spiritual need. Each individual needs to love and be loved. "The greatest of these is [love]" (I Cor. 13:13).
C. God is love. The more of Him we have, the more love we possess. Prayer, reading God's Word, total surrender to His will, and sharing His love with others brings more of His love to us. We can become "spiritual millionaires" (I Tim. 6:17-19).

16

Tests to Determine God's Will

"Wherefore be ye not unwise, but understanding what the will of the Lord is" (Eph. 5:17).

Many Christians have difficulty finding and knowing God's will for their lives. They need to take the following tests.

I. The Prayer Test

"But in every thing by prayer . . . let your requests be made known unto God" (Phil. 4:6).

  A. Prayer is the first step. Everything must be brought to God and laid before Him in complete and total surrender.
  B. As we pray, the Holy Spirit confirms God's will to us with a feeling of rightness and sureness (see I Thess. 5:17-18).

II. The Promise Test

"Whereby are given unto us exceeding great and precious promises" (II Peter 1:4).

  A. The Bible may not give specific rules for each detail of life, but God's great principles can be applied to every important course of action.
  B. Many fail to know God's will because they fail to consult His Word. We must study, search, accept the promises, and apply God's principles to our situations (II Cor. 1:20).

III. The Purpose Test

"The things that I purpose, do I purpose according to the flesh . . . ?" (II Cor. 1:17).

  A. In our quest for God's will, purpose is of utmost importance. We must abandon pride, resentment, and personal desires.

B. Selfish motives must go. We must seek only to glorify God and do those things that are pleasing to Him (Ps. 17:3).

IV. The Patience Test
"Wait on the LORD: be of good courage, and he shall strengthen thine heart" (Ps. 27:14).
A. Waiting can be most difficult. We want things to happen immediately.
B. Satan's strategy is to get Christians to rush in where angels fear to tread. We must wait for God to reveal His will. His timing is always right (Isa. 40:31).

V. The Providence Test
"I will go before thee, and make the crooked places straight" (Isa. 45:2).
A. Some wait for the big chance that never comes. When God opens a small door, enter. You may find abundant opportunity for service and blessings.
B. When God reveals His will to His own, He always goes before and makes a way. The providence of God works in conjunction with His will (Isa. 41:18).

17

How to Win Over S-E-L-F

"Then said Jesus . . . If any man will come after me, let him deny himself, and take up his cross, and follow me" (Matt. 16:24).

Perhaps the greatest battle with which most Christians must cope has to do with self. The following will help us win over S-E-L-F.

I. S-urrender All to Christ

". . . but yield yourselves unto God . . ." (Rom. 6:13).

A. Many Christians fail to surrender all to Christ. They live defeated lives because they try to accomplish too much on their own strength.

B. We must depend on Jesus Christ, putting implicit faith and trust in Him. We must let Him help carry our burdensome load and share the responsibilities in our lives.

C. The Holy Spirit enables the totally committed to win over self. This is our "reasonable service" (Rom. 12:1).

II. E-ndure Hardship for Christ

"Thou therefore endure hardness, as a good soldier of Jesus Christ" (II Tim. 2:3).

A. A good soldier endures hardship for his home and country. He must always be prepared to face the heat of battle.

B. Good soldiers of Jesus Christ must endure hardship for Him. They must take their stand for Christ and withstand persecution.

C. If we suffer for Christ we will reign with him and have victory (II Tim. 2:12). This victory will include victory over self.

III. L-ove Others as Christ

". . . the Son of God, who loved me, and gave himself for me" (Gal. 2:20).

   A. Some Christians do not sufficiently love God and others, their main concern is for personal gain.

   B. Christ lived a selfless life and died a selfless death. He lived to help others and died to save them.

   C. If we are to win over self, we must love others. "If we love one another, God dwelleth in us, and his love is perfected in us" (I John 4:12).

IV. F-aithfully Serve with Christ

"We then, as workers together with him . . ." (II Cor. 6:1).

   A. Many Christians are unfruitful because they are unfaithful in their service for God. Involvement in their own affairs causes neglect and carelessness.

   B. We win over self by working together with Christ. He will assist us as we help the less fortunate, visit the sick, and witness to the unsaved.

   C. If we serve faithfully with Christ in this life, we shall live eternally with Him in the life to come. "Be thou faithful unto death, and I will give thee a crown of life" (Rev. 2:10).

18

The Face of Jesus

"And was transfigured before them: and his face did shine as the sun, and his raiment was white as the light" (Matt. 17:2).

Let us note some of the aspects of the face of Jesus so we can better emulate Him.

I. A Purposeful Face

"He stedfastly set his face to go to Jerusalem" (Luke 9:51).

   A. Jesus came to earth for a purpose—to die for our sins. His earthly life was entirely focused on Calvary's cross.
   B. Satan, through wicked men, tried to dissuade Jesus from His goal, but not even mighty men could stop Him.
   C. We also must set our face toward a purpose. Our goal should be to make heaven. No matter whether some hate us or trials beset us, we must not be diverted from our goal (Matt. 10:22).

II. A Prayerful Face

"And he went a little farther, and fell on his face, and prayed . . ." (Matt. 26:39).

   A. Jesus sometimes bowed his head while praying, but He often lifted His face toward heaven while communing with His Father.
   B. Through prayer Jesus received strength to endure testing. He was anointed to heal the sick, give sight to the blind, comfort the lonely, and forgive sins.
   C. Prayer enables us to withstand temptation and empowers us for service (Matt. 21:22).

III. A Persecuted Face
"Then did they spit in his face, and buffeted him" (Matt. 26:67).
- A. Man deserved to die for his sins, "For the wages of sin is death," but Jesus paid the penalty. "The gift of God is eternal life through Jesus Christ our Lord" (Rom. 6:23).
- B. Jesus suffered insult, ridicule, and humiliation, but He never strayed from His purpose of living and dying for us.
- C. We also must withstand persecution, "Yea, and all that will live godly . . . shall suffer persecution" (II Tim. 3:12). We must persevere as Jesus did.

IV. A Praiseworthy Face
"And they shall see his face; and his name shall be in their foreheads" (Rev. 22:4).
- A. Loved ones work long hours and sacrifice to provide for their families. They deserve our love and appreciation.
- B. Yet Jesus' love and self-denial is far greater than any man's. No human effort could atone for our sins. Only Christ's sacrifice was efficacious.
- C. Christians grow anxious to be reunited with loved ones gone on to be with Jesus. But the greatest joy in heaven will be seeing Jesus and looking on His face. There we shall revel in His love eternally (Isa. 35:10).

19

The Love of Money

"For the love of money is the root of all evil" (I Tim. 6:10).

There is no sin in having money. However, loving money more than God or others is wrong. Our attitude and use of money makes the difference.

I. **Some Live for Money**

   "We brought nothing into this world, and it is certain we can carry nothing out" (I Tim. 6:7).

   A. Some live for money, hoarding, hiding, and worshipping wealth. They act like they expect to take it with them into the next world, but "it is certain we can carry nothing out."
   B. Countless numbers sacrifice friends, family, and spiritual health for money. The love of money distorts their values (I Tim. 6:10).
   C. The more miserly people become, the less happy they are.

II. **Some Lust After Money**

   "They that will be rich fall . . . into many foolish and hurtful lusts . . ." (I Tim. 6:9).

   A. Some set their affections on money. Their purpose in life is to get rich at any cost (Ps. 49:16-17).
   B. Many people lie, cheat, steal, and kill for money. It is the "root of all evil."
   C. Through his subtlety, Satan tempts Christians to become more and more desirous of money. We must remember "the serpent beguiled Eve through his subtilty . . ." (II Cor. 11:3).

III. Some Lose Through Money

"They have erred from the faith, and pierced themselves through with many sorrows" (I Tim. 6:10).

A. The Great Depression of the '30s brought devastation. Many lost their life savings. Some committed suicide because of this loss.//
B. Multitudes of people have lost their homes, health, and honor because they trusted in uncertain riches instead of the living God (I Tim. 6:17).//
C. A lost soul is the saddest loss of all. "For what shall it profit a man, if he shall gain the whole world, and lose his own soul?" (Mark 8:36).

IV. Some Lift with Money

"That they be rich in good works, ready to distribute, willing to communicate" (I Tim. 6:18).

A. When and if riches come, we must not set our affections on them. Rather, we must "trust in . . . God, who giveth us richly all things to enjoy" (I Tim. 6:17).//
B. God is pleased when we use our money to lift the needy, ill, and aged.//
C. Christians should generously support God's kingdom on earth, "Laying up in store for themselves a good foundation against the time to come, that they may lay hold on eternal life" (I Tim. 6:19).

20

How to L-E-A-N on Jesus

"Casting all your care upon him; for he careth for you"
(I Peter 5:7).

Today's sinful and dangerous world demands that Christians learn how to L-E-A-N on Jesus. The following outline shows us how.

I. L-ook to Jesus

"Looking unto Jesus the author and finisher of our faith . . ."
(Heb. 12:2).

- A. Many Christians put their security in others. They become upset and discouraged when the faults and failures of these others become apparent.
- B. Some love money and look to temporal pursuits for security. Frustration and insecurity ensue when money is insufficient and temporal pursuits don't satisfy.
- C. When we keep our eyes on Jesus, we are enabled to lean on Him, thus finding real and lasting security. Jesus never fails (Matt. 6:33).

II. E-ndure for Jesus Patiently

"After he [Abraham] had patiently endured, he obtained the promise" (Heb. 6:15).

- A. Many accept Christ as Savior but fail to take their stand for him. When trials and testings strike, they give up in despair.
- B. Abraham endured patiently and obtained what God had promised. We too, are to trust in God with patience, no matter what may happen.
- C. After Pentecost, the Holy Spirit enabled Peter to withstand persecution. He will help us stand, too. Those who endure to the end are assured of eternal life (Matt. 10:22).

III. A-sk of Jesus Confidently

"The confidence . . . that, if we ask any thing according to his will, he heareth us" (I John 5:14).

A. When children ask, they expect to receive from their parents. They ask persistently until they do.
B. Many Christians pray but they do not ask in faith. Prayers of faith please God and receive answers.
C. We have confidence that if we ask according to His will we shall receive. We can lean on Jesus knowing that everything is working together for good (Rom. 8:28).

IV. N-estle Close to Jesus Trustingly

"Submit yourselves therefore to God . . . Draw nigh to God, and he will draw nigh to you" (James 4:7-8)

A. Some Christians fail to commit themselves totally to God. They reserve a portion, or portions, of their lives for themselves.
B. We must yield our all to God without reservation. Prayer, Bible reading, and the expression of our love for Him in countless other ways bring us closer to God.
C. "He will draw nigh to you." As we nestle close to Jesus, we can lean on Him in sunshine and rain, joy and sorrow, and life and death (Prov. 3:5-6).

21

The Prodigal Son

"For this my son was dead, and is alive again; he was lost, and is found. And they began to be merry" (Luke 15:24).

The prodigal son is a figure of those who spurn God's love for temporal pursuits. They, too, can be restored.

I. The Spurning

"Give me the portion of goods that falleth to me. . . . And took his journey into a far country . . . " (Luke 15:12-13).

A. The prodigal son left his home—shelter, food, clothing, love, and affection—because he became discontented.

B. The prodigal son spurned the love of his father. His self-will caused him to leave without yielding to reason. He was stubborn and possessed by wanderlust.

C. Vast numbers today spurn God's love. They forsake His house, His people, and His love. Like the prodigal son, they take their journey into the far country of sin and disgrace.

II. The Learning

"And when he had spent all . . . he began to be in want . . . and no man gave unto him" (Luke 15:14-16).

A. When the prodigal had wealth, he was popular. After losing his money, he also lost his friends.

B. Wanting, wretched, and wasted, "no man gave unto him." Sinful pleasures always end in misery. They cannot satisfy the longing soul.

C. Unrepented and repeated sin brings death to body, mind, and soul. But Jesus Christ can lift the penitent soul out of the depths of despair.

III. The Yearning

"And when he came to himself, he said . . . I will arise and go to my father . . ." (Luke 15:17-19).

A. Adversity brought the prodigal son to his senses. Friends, money, and self-respect were gone. Dirty, broken, condemned, he felt like the most undeserving person on earth.

B. As he yearned for home, he was ready to say, "Father, I am no more worthy to be called thy son: make me as one of thy hired servants."

C. The sinner must want God more than anything else. Like the prodigal, he must recognize his unworthiness.

IV. The Returning

"And he arose, and came to his father . . ." (Luke 15:20-24).

A. What a welcome the prodigal son received! The welcome began even before he reached home and confessed and repented of his sins. He received compassion, love, and forgiveness.

B. The best robe which was reserved for special honors, a ring for the mark of dignity, shoes to distinguish the free from the slave, and the fatted calf for the feast to celebrate his return—all were his.

C. God gives the penitent soul the welcome of his life (here and eternally). "For this my son was dead, and is alive again; he was lost, and is found" (Luke 15:24).

22

The Road to Spiritual Success

"For then thou shalt make thy way prosperous, and then thou shalt have good success" (Josh. 1:8)

Spiritual success should be the goal of every Christian. The following points will assist the truly sincere in their quest.

I. Walk in God's Way
"This is the way, walk ye in it . . ." (Isa. 30:21).
- A. Ever so many people are going their own way. They are wasting their life seeking sinful pleasures and selfish pursuits (II Peter 3:3).
- B. God's way leads to salvation. When we confess our sins and commit our life to Christ, we receive His forgiveness and heart cleansing (I John 1:9).
- C. To walk in God's way brings peace, contentment, and spiritual success in this life, plus eternal joy in the life to come (Eph. 5:1-2).

II. Watch What You Say
"Even so the tongue is a little member . . . how great a matter a little fire kindleth!" (James 3:15).
- A. Some Christians are careless in what they say. Their talk is dominated by criticism and negativism.
- B. Careless words can discourage, depress, and destroy. God will judge Christians for their words as well as their deeds (Matt. 12:36-37).
- C. Kindness, understanding, and optimism bring healing to others, glory to God, and spiritual success to oneself (Eph. 4:32).

III. Wait When You Pray

"Wait on the LORD: be of good courage . . . wait, I say, on the LORD" (Ps. 27:14).

A. It often takes time for God to answer our prayers.
B. But many Christians are unwilling to wait God's time. They want immediate answers. When forced to wait, these Christians become plagued with doubt and discouragement.
C. We must be prepared to wait when we pray. Praising the Lord while we wait for His will to be done brings spiritual success (Ps. 40:3).

IV. Work While It Is Day

"I must work the works of him that sent me, while it is day: the night cometh . . ." (John 9:4).

A. Many Christians are lethargic about doing God's work. Jesus urged us to work now "while it is day."
B. This is our day of opportunity. We must labor with diligence. "The night cometh, when no man can work" (John 9:4).
C. Helping the less-fortunate, visiting the sick and lonely, and sharing Christ with the unsaved bring spiritual success both now and later (Matt. 16:27).

23

Your Life Is a Voyage

"So he bringeth them unto their desired haven" (Ps. 107:30).

Life is a voyage that is sometimes calm and uneventful but at other times is racked by trials. To make the journey successful . . .

I. Take Christ as Your Captain

"For it became him . . . to make the captain of their salvation perfect through sufferings" (Heb. 2:10).

   A. A ship without a captain is doomed to frustration and failure.

   B. Christ is our Captain. He keeps the soul when the billows roll. We must take our orders from Him (Heb. 2:10).

II. Take the Bible as Your Chart

"Thy word is a lamp unto my feet, and a light unto my path" (Ps. 119:105).

   A. If a ship is to arrive at its desired destination, a chart is necessary to guide its course.

   B. The Word of God is the Christian's chart. To arrive safely in heaven's port, we must follow the Bible route.

III. Take the Holy Spirit as Your Compass

"When he, the Spirit of truth, is come, he will guide you into all truth" (John 16:13).

   A. Without a compass, the ship would suffer from lack of proper direction.

   B. The Holy Spirit guides Christians safely through this life. He will guide the totally committed into all truth (John 16:13).

IV. Take Faith as Your Cable

"Now faith is the substance of things hoped for, the evidence of things not seen" (Heb. 11:1).

A. The cable extends under the water from the ship to the anchor. It keeps the ship from drifting out to sea and being lost.

B. Our spiritual cable (faith) must be kept intact. Winds and waves cannot divert us from our course. Storms and stress cannot destroy us if our cable is strong and sure.

V. Take Hope as Your Anchor (Constancy)

"Which hope we have as anchor of the soul, both sure and stedfast . . ." (Heb. 6:19).

A. When the anchor of a ship fails, the cable is useless also. The ship may be lost.

B. Hope is the Christian's spiritual anchor; it is attached to faith. When the anchor of hope fails, then faith also becomes ineffective. We must hope constantly (Ps. 42:5, 11).

VI. Take Love as Your Companion ("God is love")

"For he hath said, I will never leave thee . . ." (Heb. 13:5).

A. Throughout their voyage on the vast ocean of life, Christians have a never-failing Companion.

B. When the waters are placid, He is there. When the storms rage, He is there to bring "them unto their desired haven" (Ps. 107:30).

24

M-O-S-E-S

"Now therefore go, and I will be with thy mouth, and teach thee what thou shalt say" (Exod. 4:12).

We do well to emulate the characteristics of Moses. His Christlike attributes are needed today by all Christians.

I. M-eekness
  A. Moses was a very humble man: " . . . meek, above all the men which were upon the face of the earth" (Num. 12:3).
  B. Jesus Christ humbled Himself to become the propitiation for our sin. "And being found in fashion as a man, he humbled himself . . ." (Phil. 2:8).
  C. God loves the humble. He hates pride (Prov. 8:13). We must work and witness in humility for Christ.

II. O-bedience
  A. Moses was successful in leading the children of Israel out of Egyptian bondage because he obeyed God's voice (Exod. 6:6).
  B. Christ " . . . became obedient unto death, even the death of the cross" (Phil. 2:8). He paid the penalty for our sins, enabling us to be set free from the bondage of sin.
  C. We must obey the Lord so we can glorify Him and be a blessing to others.

III. S-ervice
  A. Moses dedicated his life to God's service. He was God's emancipator, bringing liberty to the children of Israel.

- B. Christ is the Great Emancipator. He heals the sick, lifts the fallen, and frees the lost from the penalty of sin (Luke 4:18).
- C. We must do service for God by assisting the needy and sharing Christ with the unsaved.

IV. E-ndurance
- A. Moses endured testings and trials to accomplish God's work. "For he endured, as seeing him who is invisible" (Heb. 11:27).
- B. Christ endured the cross to bring the plan of salvation down to mankind (Heb. 12:2-3).
- C. We also must endure hardships that we may be able to bring others to Christ.

V. S-acrifice
- A. Moses was willing to die to atone for the sins of the children of Israel. "Forgive their sin—; and if not, blot me, I pray thee, out of thy book . . ." (Exod. 32:32).
- B. Christ paid the supreme price for our sins. "After he had offered one sacrifice for sins for ever, sat down on the right hand of God" (Heb. 10:12).
- C. We, too, must deny ourselves. We must give of our time, talent, and treasure to build God's kingdom here on earth.

25

Stop Fretting

"Fret not thyself because of evildoers, neither be thou envious against the workers of iniquity" (Ps. 37:1).

Fretting is displeasing to God. It hinders the Christian's influence. It saps his peace of mind. Christians who do the following will be enabled to stop fretting.

I. Rely on the Lord

"Trust in the LORD, and do good . . ." (Ps. 37:3).

A. Many Christians rely too much on self-effort and fail. Human strength is insufficient for today's needs (Prov. 3:5).

B. Many lean too heavily on others even though finite ability often fails.

C. Depend on the infinite power of God. He will help us stop fretting and become the blessing we should be.

II. Rejoice in the Lord

"Delight thyself also in the LORD . . ." (Ps. 37:4).

A. Most Christians fail to look for the good. They continue to fret about people and situations.

B. Deliberate action must be taken to rejoice, especially when adversity strikes. The apostle Paul admonished Christians to "Rejoice in the Lord always" (Phil. 4:4).

C. One cannot rejoice and fret at the same time. Fretting never helps; rejoicing does. Why then don't we rejoice more?

III. Relinquish to the Lord
"Commit thy way unto the LORD . . ." (Ps. 37:5).
- A. A stubborn will hinders a Christian's outreach. We impede our usefulness when we insist on doing things our own way.
- B. We cannot control the events or people of this world. Therefore, let us stop fretting and relinquish all to God (Prov. 3:6).
- C. We need to make a total commitment to God. Let go and let Him do His work through us. Let Him bear the responsibility. He can bring it to pass.

IV. Rest in the Lord
"Rest in the LORD, and wait patiently for him" (Ps. 37:7).
- A. Impatience is damaging to the Christian's tranquility. "In your patience possess ye your souls" (Luke 21:19).
- B. Rest in the Lord. Recognize and practice the presence of God daily, moment by moment.
- C. Rely on the Lord. Rejoice in the Lord. Relinquish to the Lord. Rest in the Lord. "And the peace of God . . . shall keep your heart and minds . . ." (Phil. 4:7).

26

The Bible Speaks

"Order my steps in thy word: and let not any iniquity have dominion over me" (Ps. 119:133).

The Bible speaks to our hearts because it is God's personal message to us.

I. **Study It**

"Give me understanding, that I may learn thy commandments" (Ps. 119:73).

  A. Many Christians fail to make spiritual progress because they neglect the study of God's Word. They may read a verse on the run, if, indeed, they read the Bible at all.
  B. Systematic methods are needed for Bible study. Commentaries and encyclopedias are valuable. Prayer and study groups, under qualified leadership, are also helpful.
  C. We must take time to study the Word of God. His promises bring salvation, serenity, strength, and stability. (Ps. 119:33-34).

II. **Store It**

"Thy word have I hid in mine heart, that I might not sin against thee" (Ps. 119:11).

  A. Some Christians fail to store God's Word in their hearts. When trouble arises, they are unable to meet the challenges.
  B. We can cope with the wiles of the devil only as we hide God's Word in our heart, for Satan goes about "as a roaring lion . . . seeking whom he may devour" (I Peter 5:8).
  C. We should read the promises, write them down, memorize them, and use them. Through them we find direction (Ps. 119:105).

III. Savor It

"Let thy tender mercies come unto me, that I may live: for thy law is my delight" (Ps. 119:77).

A. Cherish the Word of God. When we partake of it daily, it actually becomes a part of us. "O taste and see that the LORD is good" (Ps. 34:8).
B. Delight in God's promises. They teach us His will for our lives. By claiming them through faith we receive miracles.
C. Thank God for giving us His Word. In it He has provided promises to meet all our needs (Ps. 119:97).

IV. Share It

"My tongue shall speak of thy word . . ." (Ps. 119:172).

A. Many Christians fail to share God's Word. Perhaps they want to keep it to themselves. This is impossible, for we keep God's Word only as we share it with others.
B. We share God's Word by assisting the poor, comforting the lonely, and telling the unsaved about Christ our Savior and Lord.
C. "I will speak of thy testimonies also before kings, and will not be ashamed" (Ps. 119:46).

27

This Is the Y-E-A-R (New Year's)

"The Spirit of the Lord is upon me, because he hath anointed me . . . To preach the acceptable year of the Lord" (Luke 4:18-19).

This is the year for every Christian to excel for God. All who accept the challenge may find this to be their best Y-E-A-R.

I. Y-ield to the Lord

". . . yield yourselves unto God, as those that are alive from the dead . . ." (Rom. 6:13).

  A. Sometimes committed Christians slacken their efforts and begin to grow spiritually lax.
  B. When this happens, they need to repent and rededicate themselves, submitting to God's will daily. They need to draw nigh to God (James 4:7-8).
  C. Christians should fully surrender themselves to God. By doing so they will become a blessing to others, gain spiritual insight, and glorify God through the coming year.

II. E-ndure for the Lord

"But watch thou in all things, endure afflictions" (II Tim. 4:5).

  A. Some Christians continually seek the easy way. When difficult situations arise, their first thought is, "How will this affect me?"
  B. Christ endured the cross, giving His life for us (Gal. 2:20). We must sacrifice for Christ, put away self-seeking and selfish desires.
  C. Strive to endure all for God. Persecution and trial will strengthen our faith (I Peter 5:10).

III. A-dvance with the Lord

"I can do all things through Christ which strengtheneth me"
(Phil. 4:13).

A. Many Christians excuse themselves from doing God's work: some are hampered by inferiorities; others are spiritually lazy.

B. Christians should keep their priorities in proper perspective by giving God first place. No reason or excuse should keep them from doing God's work.

C. Begin now to advance the kingdom of God this year (II Cor. 6:1) through work, prayer, trust, and obedience.

IV. R-ejoice in the Lord

"Rejoice in the Lord alway: and again I say, Rejoice"
(Phil. 4:4).

A. Some Christians' negative attitudes rob them of the joy that salvation affords.

B. Our world is filled with sin, sadness, and sorrow, but Christ came to bring hope and joy. Joy is attractive and people will go where it can be found.

C. Christians should overflow with rejoicing in the Lord. Forgiveness, cleansing, and the hope of eternal life bring joy here and now, plus everlasting life to come (Isa. 35:10). Rejoice in the Lord and make this your happiest year.